MAISIE AND ME

*Cover: View towards Westbury White Horse drawn by
Simon Jones from an old postcard lent by
Wiltshire Library and Museum Service.
Inset: Maisie (below) and Stella Ashton (above).*

MAISIE
& ME

*A Country Childhood
in the 1920s*

Stella Ashton

Illustrations by Malcolm Joseph

EX LIBRIS PRESS

First published in 1992 by
Ex Libris Press
1 The Shambles
Bradford on Avon
Wiltshire

Typeset in 11 point Century Schoolbook and Palatino

Design and typesetting by Ex Libris Press

Cover printed by Shires Press, Trowbridge
Printed and bound in Great Britain by
Cromwell Press Ltd., Broughton Gifford, Wiltshire

ISBN 0 948578 51 3

To the third generation:
Oliver, Megan, Rachel, Alexander and Elizabeth

CONTENTS

About the Author   7

Maisie and Me   9
    Our Village; Bratton and its Bees; Rape of the
    Cowslips; Cows in the Meadow; My Dream; In the
    Fever Hospital; How we both rode on the Same
    Bicycle; Mud Pies and Chalk Cakes

Work on the Farm   15
    Milking; Leading Horses; Harvest; Staddle Stones
    and the Granary; Haymaking; I get Carried Away;
    Fruit Picking; The Walnut Tree; Stuck up a Tree;
    Gypsies; Hedgehog for Dinner; Threshing;Shepherd
    and Shepherd's Hut; Shearing; The Sheep Fair;
    Motherless Lambs; Sheep-Dogs; Pip Shows his
    Obedience; A Farmer Kind to Animals; Dad Shooting;
    Foxes; Huge Straw Wagons   32

Maisie and me at School
    Our Pink Aprons; Black Bibles; Sums or no Dinner;
    The Cane;Planes on the Plain; To School by Pony
    Cart; Tragedy in the Sand Pit

Games   38
    Hop, Skip and Jump; Skipping Rhymes; Hopscotch;
    Whip Top; Ball on the Wall; Swings

The Seasons   41
    Primroses; Bird's Nesting; Swallows and Plovers;
    Pied Wagtails and Cuckoos; Pigeons; I Feed a
    Fledgling; The Crow Mimic; Dancing the Polka;

Mushrooms; Lovely Food; Picking Watercress and
Counting the Church Steps; Blackberrying; Nutting;
Stained Faces; Sunday School Picnic; Sunday School
Anniversary; The Limits of Teetotalism; Missionaries
and Magic Lanterns

Christmas   55

Classy Christmas Puddings; A Fiery Father Christmas; Dad's Feast; A Bony Ghost; A Potato in our
Stockings; Hide and Seek in the Dark

Valued Animals and Precious Characters   61

Animals our Constant Companions; Pig Killing;
Horses; Ploughman's Lunch; The Bull; A Wild White
Wyandotte; Sozzled Cock; Fishing for Tiddlers; Cold
Water; Gentleman Jack; The Bird Scarer; The Black-
smith; The White Horse; Village Characters; Fires
and Fire Engines; Looking into Reeves's Works;
Shopping Visits to Town

War and Peace   77

Our Military Invasion; Shining Soldiers; The Peace
Play

Glossary   79

About the Author

Stella Ashton was born on 23rd. March 1917, at Fussells Lodge Farm, Clarendon – on the down overlooking Salisbury. Some time later her father moved to take over the tenancy of Grange Farm, Bratton, and most of these stories of her childhood are from there. She was keen that her grandchildren should know what life was like in a fairly typical village in the twenties.

Later, Stella trained in poultry husbandry at Swanley Agricultural College, Kent, and worked on poultry farms in Sussex and Devon. During the 1939-45 war, she became poultry adviser under the Pembrokeshire County Council; then in 1946 joined the Minstry of Agriculture Advisory Service and was posted to North Devon.

She had to give up her job in 1950 (it was not, even as recently as that, permissible to be a mother and a civil servant); her first son was born that autumn and she also has a daughter, with a total of five grandchildren.

She moved to Cardiff when her partner, also in the Advisory Service, was posted there in 1951. She spent most of the rest of her life there, apart from a few years in Leeds in the sixties.

Stella died not many months after finishing these stories, in October 1992.

Grange Farm
- as it is now

Maisie and Me

Our Village

The steep chalk escarpment falls down to the greensand and gault along the northern edge of Salisbury Plain. The velvety green 'hanging', along which the shadows race in fine weather, forms the background to the villages at the foot. Chalk streams burst forth, tamed through the years in their stone-banked courses, to wind their way between the houses. The villages were mostly a huddle or perhaps a couple of streets of houses; the older ones a mellow orangey brick, the newer in redder brick, and a few have old timber frames and thatch. The landscape in the valley of hedged meadows and woods is as different from the bare hill-top as it could possibly be – well, as different as chalk from cheese!

Through the haze of years of a long lifetime I see these villages as they were at another watershed following the First World War when most of the traffic was still horse-drawn, and radio, television and atom bombs still in the future. It was within this setting that my sister Maisie and me lived at the Grange Farm in the village of Bratton and had a wonderful childhood.

Our childhood was not one of deprivation, such as I know my grandmother's had been, brought up in a cottage on Salisbury Plain. Ours was one of plenty; plenty of food, meats, vegetables, puddings, cakes, jams, honey. My mother was an excellent cook. As she was also a seamstress we had plenty of clothes too. Muslin and tussore silk in the summer and wool and velvet in the winter. However, we were not allowed to be waited on, nor were we allowed to escape our share of the work to be done.

The section of the village to which we belonged was undoubtedly possessed by the Protestant work ethic. (Of course we never had any idea at the time that that was what it would come to be called.) Without doubt most people felt that one's life should consist of days full of steady work all the hours of daylight, except, of course, on Sunday, which was a day of rest with strictly necessary work only. The fact that our enlightened parents allowed our active play to be our form of labour enabled us to have plenty of playtime alongside our real work.

Our grandmother, who lived in a neighbouring cottage, thought we had too soft a life and would stump upstairs in our house before we were up. With each step her foot went down harder on the stair and in a loud voice she would say, "Shake off dull sloth and *early* rise". In vain did we shout from our beds, "It isn't *Early* rise Gran, its *Joyful* rise – we can't be joyful as early as this!"

Bratton and its Bees

Bratton was full of little winding 'lanes' which criss-crossed the village, and of bees, gardens and orchards full of splendid fruit, for which, no doubt, the bees were largely responsible. The winding lanes enabled us children on our way to school to pick green gooseberries, ripe cherries or apples and chomp them with equal relish, without attracting anybody's attention. In May and June the sound of huge black iron door keys banging on shovels meant a swarm was settling in a tree and would shortly be smoked out and dropped into a skip for transfer to a hive. Everybody knew that a swarm of bees in May was worth a load of hay and a swarm of bees in June was worth a silver spoon, even if most of the cottagers involved rarely had a load of hay and never a silver spoon!

Rape of the Cowslips

It was spring and early summer when the 'lords and ladies' (arum lilies) beckoned colourfully, aggressively and dangerously from the banks and hedgerows, and when our parents' persistent poison warnings stopped us from gathering them, that we turned in compensation to the meadows and gathered straw bags full of cowslip heads for Mrs. Smith's wine-making. This was not a quiet gathering, with long stalks and longer sniffs at their perfume which we accorded the first primroses in February, but a churlish pulling off of heads and stuffing these into bags until one could not open them without having the flower heads all come springing out. The rape of the cowslips always left me with a sad, painful feeling, not assuaged by Mrs. Smith's, "Oh, thank you my dears, that is a lovely lot."

Cows in the Meadow

May too was the time for turning the cows out into the grassy meadows of Cap's Lane. The long trail of short-horn cows – strawberry roan, snowball white and almost orange-red in colour – slowly wended their way from the cow shed and yards where they had spent the winter and sauntered along, cropping the roadside grasses en route, until their own five-barred gate came into view. The child cowherd then rushed ahead of them to throw the gate open, and they all immediately put on a spurt to get through the gate together to the lush, green, waiting grass. No chemical sprays had removed the buttercups and they set off the green sward with their beautiful gold petals.

My Dream

One May when I had scarlet fever and was hauled off to the local isolation hospital, my fevered dream was of lying in that green meadow amongst the buttercups and then slowly, dreamily taking the cows home for milking. When I awoke in the white polished ward with white polished nurses calling me, scalding tears flowed down onto my nightie, but the dream has remained vivid for almost seventy years!

In the Fever Hospital

My sister Maisie and I were together in this hospital along with lots of other children in one of the epidemics which occurred in those days. We had to stay isolated for six weeks, but when we were better we played together in the hospital field. This field was the habitat of a great many types and colours of butterflies. When a butterfly settled on a plant we dropped our linen hats over it, but we did not kill it; we soon picked up the hat and let it fly away. Next to the hospital field was a large wire-netting pen full of turkeys. We children, perhaps fifteen or more, would hold hands and, marching up to the fence in a long line, would chant in loud voices interspersed with guffaws of laughter, "What d'you hang your father with?", and the turkeys would answer with the only word they knew, "'alter, 'alter, 'alter." I think this made me suspicious of plebiscites and referenda for life, for ask a loaded question and the answer is inevitable, even for turkeys!

How we both Rode on the Same Bicycle

Maisie and I were a couple of red-headed, freckle-faced girls living on a lovely old Wiltshire farm. We were great pals and about the same size, shape and weight at the time I remember, even though Maisie was three years older than me. How do I know that? Because we used to ride together on one bicycle. Nothing unusual about that you may think, but we rode one on each pedal, propelling the bicycle in this way, Maisie guiding with the handlebars and me holding on to the saddle, our two ginger heads bobbing up and down as we rushed along. This, of course, must have been illegal even in those days, but in the country lanes there was very little traffic.

Mud Pies and Chalk Cakes

We lived in chalk country, and this featured strongly in all our play. Some days, in the school holidays, we made 'iced cakes' and set them out on stalls. The 'cakes' we made of the stiff local clay and turned them out in shapes. After this we ground up a piece of chalk and made for each one a wonderful 'icing', decorating them with small, brightly coloured flowers; celandine, golden yellow; scarlet pimpernel, bright red, harebell, deep blue, and so on. The 'cakes' which we sold to each other and our friends for flint stone money quickly dried up and then we had a great game shying them at the barn doors. Making and decorating the cakes was just as much fun next time it became the day's play.

Work on the Farm

At the time of which I write the type of farming was of the four course rotation with the sheep flock as an integral part of it. The sheep flock ate off the root crop and manured the soil on the Plain and this enabled oats, barley or wheat crop or a grass ley to be grown. This went round in a rotation. Not long after this period, in the thirties in fact, this system collapsed because of the slump in sheep, wool and grain prices, and most hill land was put down to grass for some years before it was broken up again in the Second World War. So the period of which I write was a watershed in farming methods and the coming to an end of the time when most farm work was carried out by horses.

Milking

Our life was not all play. Although then only about nine to twelve-years-old we did quite a lot of work. During harvest, when all the men were busy, we brought in from the meadows a herd of cows and hand-milked them. Sometimes our rather older cousins helped. There was fun as we squirted milk into each other's mouths. One couldn't always hit the mouth of course, so the milk might go into an eye or down the neck! There was fear as we approached a cow who was a known kicker. Sometimes the three-legged stool on which we sat, and us with it, would go flying into the straw. One day a cow upped and put her dirty hoof right into a pail of milk, but I don't remember that happening often. The cows all had names, not numbers such as they have now. There was Snowball, Bluebell, Buttercup, Strawberry and even one poor cow who was just called John. Why she was given such an unsuitable name of the wrong gender, I don't know. The names did on the whole reflect the colours of the cows in a shorthorn herd.

Leading Horses

On other days at the height of the corn harvest, Maisie and I used to work out in the harvest field. One of us would lead the wagon horses from stook to stook, or 'hiles' as we called them. There would be a man on each side of the wagon and he would pitch the sheaves up to a loader, often a boy. The men wanted to keep on pitching all the time so we had to watch closely and lead on the horses as soon as the sheaves were up. The other one of us would lead in the horses with a fully loaded wagon into the stack where an elevator was kept working, and several men building the huge oblong corn-stack in the field to await threshing later.

Harvest

Sometimes we would take part in the making of the 'hiles' with the men, and woe betide you if you didn't plant your two sheaves just at the same time as your partner to make the stook stand up properly. If it had been damp in the night and the sheaves were not stooked, our father would have us go down the rows and turn over all the sheaves so that the sun and wind could dry them. Oh, the field seemed to stretch on forever when we had to do this. Lunch-time and tea-time usually meant that someone came up from the farm bearing a basketful of sandwiches and a white enamel can full of hot, sweet milky tea for everyone to share.

Staddle Stones and the Granary

The granary at the Grange Farm was a beautiful old wooden building that stood on staddle stones. There were any number of these staddle stones around. The staddle stone consists of two pieces, the stem and the cap. They are like large mushrooms. The stem is about two feet in height and the cap perhaps just a little under two feet in diameter. They were arranged to carry the timbers of the granary on the caps so that no rodent could possibly penetrate the granary and foul the beautiful golden grain stored in it. Of course, the door must never be left open, and woe betide anyone who left a fork or rake standing against the outside walls, as this would immediately allow a rat to climb up and gnaw its way in.

The granary was such a special place that nobody was allowed in unless my Dad was there. I felt an enormous privilege at standing inside and could not have been more awestruck had the piles of grain been, in fact, piles of gold. There were occasions, after the harvest, when father put samples of that golden grain into little hessian sacks and took them to Devizes market to make sales of our precious product.

Haymaking
Haymaking was fun too, but not so much as harvest. Although the smell of new-mown hay was redolent of high summer, who would swap it for the smell of silage? We quickly learned to use horse-rakes and side-rakes and put the hay into swathes.

I get Carried Away
My father had a hay-loader, which is an elevator-type machine hitched behind a wagon. It has hooks on it which grab the hay from the swathe after which it travels up the elevator and empties onto the wagon. One day, thinking it would be fun to ride up the elevator

with that hay, I hitched my tough cotton overall to one of the hooks. I started to rise up with the hay, then fear gripped me and I had to shout for Dad, who was in front of the wagon leading the horse, to stop and get me down. He was horrified when he saw what was happening as it would have been very dangerous. I never did confess that I did it on purpose.

Fruit Picking

Apple-picking was a wonderful time. The Grange Farm at that time had two magnificent orchards and, probably because the village of Bratton had so many cottage bee-keepers, the fruit both in yield and quality was as fine as I have ever seen. From the earliest 'Beauty of Bath' in July to the autumn 'Orange Blenheims' and 'Russets', the orchards were a wonderful source of jolly work and succulent nourishment. Most of the trees were 'standards' in those days, so it was necessary to climb up a ladder to pick the apples. We usually had a hessian bag slung across one shoulder with binder-twine and hanging down one side so that you had both hands free. Then you started to pick, very gently lowering the apples into the bag. There were, of course, plum trees and pear trees as well, though fewer of these than apples.

When the apples were picked, the bushel baskets were carried over to the farmhouse and laid out on straw in a big room upstairs which had previously been the Cheese Room and was still called that. There they made the most beautiful piles, the keepers separated from the non-keepers or short-keepers. Many of them lasted until March of the following year. Sometimes my father sold a tree of apples or plums to a fruit dealer. One day when we were cheerfully picking and sometimes eating plums from a blue plum tree, the dealer came into the orchard and announced that he had bought the whole plum-tree crop. We sorrowfully got down from the tree leaving our pickings behind, but glad that we could not hand back the plums in our tummies.

The Walnut Tree

In the lower orchard there was a range of pigsties with corrugated iron roofs housing three of four sows almost always with a litter of piglets. The back of the pigsty was under a huge walnut tree, so we climbed on to the roof and knocked down walnuts when we thought they were getting ripe. Getting them out of the outer green casing was impossible without getting one's hands and mouth stained brown. Thereby hangs the tale of the way Maisie and I and a friend decided to turn ourselves into gypsies for a day by staining our faces deliberately – but more about that later!

Stuck up a Tree

Before we leave the orchards I have one more memory of Maisie and me in our dinner hour from school – climbing, without a ladder, one of the taller apple trees.

When it was nearly two o'clock, the time we had to be back at school, Maisie climbed down and dropped the last ten foot or so onto the turf and ran off to school. I could not make the last drop as it seemed an enormous way down, that is, not until I heard the two o'clock hooter sound for the Agricultural Implement Works. I knew I should catch it if I was late for school so I just fell out of the tree with an almighty bump and, rubbing my bruises, dashed off to school with the speed of lightning.

Gypsies

Well, talking of looking like gypsies reminds me that gypsies often impinged on our lives. They lived in horse-drawn caravans up on Salisbury Plain, and came into the villages to collect rabbit skins and sell clothes-pegs. Often in the summer the gypsy children, who would be clustering around their mother, had no shoes on. They were the only children in our village who went barefoot. We were half afraid of them, probably remembering stories of being taken to live with the gypsies. For all that, we would shout after them as they toiled up the long chalk tracks to the down – 'Diddicoys' – and then run away in case they really had heard us.

My father had a mass of stories about the gypsies. He farmed land up on the Plain, miles away from the farmhouse. Turnips and swedes were grown there for the sheep flock and, not unnaturally, when no one was around the gypsies helped themselves to these good vegetables. I was up on the Plain in the milk-float with father one day when he suddenly ducked down and ran off half-bent till he was out of sight, leaving me with the horse and float. I must have been seven or eight years old at the time and I was very frightened and started to wail and cry. After a bit Dad came back very angry. "What did you make that noise for?", he demanded. "I was just about to catch a fellow stealing my turnips, but you frightened him off."

Hedgehog for Dinner

On another occasion when father was moving gypsies off his land, he noticed they were gathered around a fire cooking something when one of the gypsies said, "ave'ee a bit of hedgehog maister", for that is what was cooking away in clay in the fire. At yet another time the gypsies were absolutley refusing to move off our land and father, who usually went around with a double-barrelled shotgun to shoot rabbits and scare crows, broke open the gun and put two cartridges in it. After this action my father said he had never seen ponies harnessed in to carts so fast! It may seem hard that the gypsies were driven off the farmers' land, but in those days they had the open Plain on which they could camp. Often this was one of the 'tynings', that is, a belt of trees on the Plain. These trees presumably furnished the wood for their clothes-pegs and for their caravan stoves.

Threshing

Maisie and I sometimes 'helped' at threshing time. Whilst some of the men cut and fed sheaves into the thresher and others staggered away with enormous hessian sacks of wheat, oats or barley as it came out in a golden stream from the threshing machine, we children and dogs gathered outside a chicken-wire fence placed all round the stack and the thresher to knock down any escaping mice or rats from the diminishing stack. The men, who were inside the wire fence, tied binder-twine round the legs of their trousers so that no escaping rodent could run up their legs. The thought of this happening terrified me and Maisie so much, and girls in those days did not wear jeans, only skirts, that we as often as not ran away at the sight of an approaching rat, which meant that it was left to the more efficient disposal of the dogs. I remember Maisie picking up a tiny mouse once, but the poor little creature just responded by biting her finger, whereupon she hastily dropped it.

Shepherd and Shepherd's Hut

One of the things Maisie and I enjoyed the most was being taken by Dad in the milk float 'up the hill', that is up on Salisbury Plain, to see the shepherd. The land was grazed by a big flock of sheep belonging to our farm. The flock was part of the rotation which was practised on those thin hill soils. The flock manured the land and the next crops of oats, wheat or barley benefitted. Shepherd – he must have had another name, but if so nobody ever used it – was in charge of the flock. He moved them around from place to place and at lambing or other busy times he lived with his sheep day and night, week in week out.

Maisie and I were always totally taken up by 'shepherd's hut', a sort of wooden shed on wheels in which he lived. It had a stove with a metal chimney pipe on one side and contained a truckle bed, a table and chair and a number of pans and mugs used for his cooking. It was warm and comfortable and we girls thought it would be the ideal place to live. However, we were unaware of the many cold spring nights when he was there completely on his own. The sheep were 'folded', that is, they were enclosed in squares of wattle hurdles to protect them from the wind and rain. Sometimes a coping of thatch made a particularly cosy corner for a lambing ewe. The strength and fitness of a farm man seemed to be measured by the number of hurdles he would carry at one time on his back. Moving folds was a lot of work. There was usually a shepherd's boy to help and possibly some of the other men. Shepherd's dog, of course, was his most treasured possession. It was a hard-working assistant and on those long, lonely nights must have been a wonderful companion.

Shearing

Shearing was also a great time when the sheep were shorn of their somewhat ragged woollen coats. Most of the shearers still used hand-shears, although there was just beginning to be machine shearing in use. One person turned the handle of the machine and another used the clippers to cut the wool. Maisie and I did not help with this work. We just stood by in wonder at the skill of the men and the tolerance of the sheep. We both tried hard to cut with the hand-shears, but they were made of a steel so strong that even with two hands we could not get the blades to cross, a movement the men did hundreds of times with one hand!

The Sheep Fair

In September of each year there was a sheep fair held on Westbury Hill, just above the White Horse, during which lots of pens of sheep were sold. Maisie and I used to look forward to going in the swinging boats which were part of the fair. She was braver than I was in pulling the ropes to make the 'boat' go higher and higher so that we could look right over the edge of the escarpment and were quite dizzied by the sight of the steep drop into the valley beyond.

Motherless Lambs

Sometimes there were motherless lambs which had to be brought up on bottles in the farm kitchen. My father had two such lambs one year which followed him everywhere. He was walking up the hill towards the sheep fair when a neighbour passing him said, "Oh, Mr. Ashton, are you taking your lambs to the sheep fair?". Then he realised that the lambs were following him. "Oh dear no," he said, "my daughters would be horrified if I did." (I suppose we must have been at school at the time). So he had to take them back home and shut them in safe from the fair.

Sheep-Dogs

My father was very good at caring for and training sheep-dogs, as he had left school at the age of twelve and become a shepherd boy herding sheep on Salisbury Plain. He insisted that the dog should be fed only one, but very good, meal a day. Of course it should have plenty of water. It should not be allowed to come into the farmhouse and sit in front of the kitchen fire, for that would prevent it from growing the thick winter coat it would need to keep warm in winter. He treated the sheep-dogs very kindly but with very firm training and discipline until obedience became absolute.

Pip Shows his Obedience

A very amusing thing happened in relation to one young dog. He had been trained never to eat anything unless given the command 'yours'. A neighbour, a fractious lady who had lived all her life in India and therefore thought that the 'locals' very much required her instruction and admonishment, came into the farmyard, took one look at the sheep-dog and said, "That animal is half-starved. You should give it more food. I will bring down a bowl of meat for it." This she duly did, and the dog – Pip was his name – looked up into her face with his brown eyes waiting for the signal that it was his, but the good lady did not know his obedience training and never gave it. The bowl of fine meat consequently remained untouched! "Well, I can hardly believe it", said the lady. "Such beautiful food too", and she went away leaving the bowl and its contents untouched on the grass. My brother, who had seen what had happened, then went over to Pip and said 'yours', and the meat disappeared in two shakes of a duck's rudder, which is to say 'pronto'. Thus was my father's regime with dogs more or less upheld, and an uppity neighbour put in her place!

A Farmer Kind to Animals

My father was kind and very considerate, if firm and unsentimental, with all of his animals. He would get out of the trap and walk beside it up the steep hill to the Plain, so that the horse should not have to carry his weight as well as mine and Maisie's. When he was bringing in milking cows from the field to milk, he would not have them hurried in any way but said that they should 'dream-along' on their walk to the byre. Once when he had just seen a huntsman whipping in the hounds he remarked with disgust, "My God, that huntsman nearly cut a hound in half with his whip."

Dad Shooting

Only on rare occasions did Maisie and I go with Dad when he was shooting. When we did we were made to stand right behind his back so that we would be in no danger. There were lots of rabbits about at that time so he shot them very frequently. Our family, like every other village family, ate lots of rabbit, which was cheap if you bought it and free if you caught it. I certainly believe that in that period of depression most country people would have been far less well nourished were it not for the rabbits. Be that as it may, my father weekly provided them for the kitchen and his boast was that he waited to get three in line so that could shoot them all with the same cartridge. When he went after hares he would hide in the grass near the hares' form and, imitating their sound, call the hares to him, only shooting when he was sure he could not miss.

When I was standing behind my father at shoots the loud bang of the gun petrified me. I quickly learnt to keep away from shoots, all that is except the rabbit catching that went on just as the binder was getting to the centre of a field of corn it was cutting. At this point rabbits started to run out by the dozen. There was usualy one very careful man with a gun, but most of the killing was done by dogs. We children used to run after rabbits escaping from the standing corn, but rarely caught them and I must say, though I joined the chase, I didn't want to catch them.

One spring morning my father was waiting for two or three rabbits to get into line so that he could shoot them all with one cartridge. Suddenly the most distant fur object rose up and was seen to be a brown felt hat on the head of a man who was bending over picking violets just below the brow of the hill. It was right out in the middle of our field a long way from any public paths, so my father was profoundly shocked and went off home without his rabbits. The violet picker never knew he had put himself in such peril!

Foxes

Maisie and I often pored over the stuffed fox that was beautifully mounted, with a pheasant in his mouth, in a glass case which stood on the hall table at the Grange Farm. This was a fox which had jumped down out of a tree when my father was haymaking in one of his meadows. He had instantly killed it with a blow from his hay-fork. Foxes were vermin and there was a continuous battle between them and the farmers. They were particularly destructive in the hen houses and poultry yards. For all that my father did not dislike them and told stories of foxy heroism, devotion and cunning.

In those days, gin-traps were still used for catching rabbits and my father saw a fox caught by one foot in a gin-trap. As he watched he saw the fox bite off his own foot and thus painfully secure its release. Another story he told us was of a dog-fox poisoned and lying dead not far from its earth. Watching over a period of several days, Dad saw the vixen regularly bring tasty morsels of food and lay them down beside her dead mate. Foxes that were being hunted he had seen depositing little bits of vomit to attract the hounds and then circling and making off in the opposite direction. In this way many must have escaped the hounds. Maisie and I felt that he gave the fox full marks for intelligence, bravery and devotion and was rather sorry he could not wholly be on its side.

Huge Straw Wagons

One sight that used to fill both Maisie and me with wonder and indeed terror was meeting big wagons of straw coming down the steep roads from the Plain. The height of these loads seemed enormous, the great bundles of yellow straw (no straw burning in those days) towered high above the lades of the wagon. Four horses, two abreast in the shafts and two in the traces, pulled it. In the steep parts of the rough stone hill road the nervous tensions of the carters showed in their shouts to the horses and when the 'drug shoes' were put on the huge wheels the metal tyres struck showers of sparks on the road. Sometimes a wagon actually turned over and shed its load, something I am sure that particular carter could never live down. Meanwhile, Maisie and I shivered together on the grassy banks of the road amidst the mauve scabious and white moon daisies, keeping well back from this scene of enormous controlled energy.

Maisie and me at School

Our school was a British School, that is, it was a school run by the chapel, all the managers being members of the chapel; and its head teacher, always called our Governess, was a prominent member of the congregation, as well, of course, as being a trained teacher. We were under the Wiltshire County Council Provision and Inspection. The other village school was a small Church of England establishment. This only ended with the building of the new Council School when the division of the village children into Chapel Kids and Church Kids ended. There was also at this time the eleven-plus scholarship, as it was called, when some village children were selected out and passed on to the High School. Most, however, remained at the elementary school until the age of fourteen.

Our Pink Aprons

Not only were Maisie and I always busy playing and working around the farm, but of course we also went to school and to Sunday school. At school it was still a time when many girls wore white aprons which looked very smart until some boy put a bit of blotting-paper into his ink-well and shot it with his steel nibbed pen at a girl's white apron. However, my mother, who was a seamstress, made Maisie and me pink aprons which we thought vastly superior, though they no doubt looked

a bit odd with our red hair. Whether the colour put the
bully-boys off I don't know, but I don't remember either
of us being the recipient of an ink shot.

Black Bibles

At school in the 'big room' – *i.e.*, the older children –
every morning as we entered our backless desks, we
would see lying on them in front of each child a big shiny
black bible. We would catch the sun's rays, if there were
any, on the shiny covers and deflect them on to other
peoples' faces until someone was caught at it by the
teacher. Each day we would read aloud a pasage from
the Bible, then write it out in our best handwriting and
finally learn it by heart. I have often surprised people
in my later non-religious life by being able to recite the
Lament of David over Jonathan, or the beautiful words
of Naomi and Ruth, or even a whole psalm. 'They that
go down to the sea in ships and do their business in
great waters,' always filled me with a wonderful feeling
of the beautiful language. Moreover I am sure that this
close and early acquaintance with the King James
version of the Bible made one feel quite at home with
Shakespeare.

Sums or no Dinner

The Bible study was followed very much by the works
of Mammon, in the form of sums about money calcu-
lations; interest, compound and simple; material
measured in yards, feet and inches, and in some in-
stances in rods, poles and perches, acres and miles.
Some sums were written down in squared exercise
books, but each morning before the lunch break there
was a session of mental arithmetic with questions from

the teacher shot out in quick fire for immediate answers. "If I have 17s.6d., to how many children could I give half-a-crown?" How many yards in a mile, feet in a chain, pints in a gallon, etc. A quick correct answer and you were allowed to go home to dinner. No answer, or a wrong one, and you sat through the quick fire questions until you got one right. I am not sure what happened if you never did because I was always gone from the room as quickly as possible. Presumably our 'governess', as we called our teacher, either tailored her questions down to the easier ones as the class thinned out, or else called 'time' so that the others, even if they couldn't do sums, could get the dinner they were pining for. I don't know whether anyone has ever done any research to show that hunger sharpens up the ability to do mental arithmetic!

The Cane

Discipline was strict in our school, but our governess was fair. On the wall hung a little knotty bamboo cane with a crook handle. It was not often used, but when it was the child had to go out in front of the whole class and hold out a hand. A very sharp whack of the cane followed, and some children would cry with pain but the heroes were those who came back to their desk smiling. Meanwhile 'Govy' had gone as red as a turkey cock and it was obvious that caning did not do any good to her blood pressure; presumably she felt it her duty to use the cane sometimes.

I have said that the cane was short, and thereby hangs another tale. It had at one time been a very long cane, but some particularly mischievous boys, who knew they were due for a caning, cut it nearly in half and then put it back on the peg. When one of them was caned the cut end flew right off and knocked off the teacher's glasses and broke them. That was the end of caning for that day.

The boys also played pranks on the teacher, such as putting a piece of dry grass on the outside of one of the window panes and then saying, "Please Miss, somebody's cracked the window." The inquisition would then take place; who had been playing cricket or football in the playground to do such a thing? No culprits came forth of course. These windows were very high up so that it was only with the use of a step ladder that you could see what had actually happened to the window. Presumably this was investigated by the caretaker after school. I think our 'Govy' got her own back for these episodes because she would often send big, mischievous, and therefore usually dirty boys to the lobby to wash themselves – hands, face, necks and knees – with cold water and carbolic soap, and to attempt to dry themselves on an ancient roller towel! Maisie and I, let me assure you, were never given the cane and certainly never sent out to wash ourselves.

Planes on the Plain

In case you should think all this took place years before it did, I will give you one story from our school which shows that the modern world was beginning to break in on it. One day, one of the boys from a 'down barn', *i.e.*, a group of barns and cottages right up on the Plain, let it be known that aeroplanes were landing 'by the hundred' just on top our our down. You must remember that most of us had never seen aeroplanes and the whole thing smacked of magic. Many children from the 'big room' made excuses to leave the room and climbed the steep chalk path to the down. There they were met by an amazing sight. Sixty three small aircraft (military of course) had landed on our down. The buzz of wonderment that went through us could not now be imagined. A sad corollary of this is that local churches and war memorials now hold the names of two or three boys we knew whose first acquaintance with aircraft must have been on that day.

To School by Pony Cart

Maisie and I had about a mile to walk to school each day which was fine as we were joined every hundred yards or so by children running out of cottages and small farms and finally converging on school together. When it was a really pouring wet day, my father had the farm boy drive us to school in the milk float pulled by the trap-horse, Sceptre. As we trotted along the road to school, children appeared from seemingly everywhere and were helped into the milk float, so that we arrived at school not just two girls in the trap, but more like a dozen kids. There was no roof or even a trap-umbrella on the float so we had to be done up in macs and sou'westers and on our feet leather boots – yes, boots. I started off with button boots which had to be done up with a button hook, but later in the winter we both had lace-up boots which came almost to the tops of our socks and fastened just below the knee.

Tragedy in the Sand Pit

Most of the experiences of children in the village in my childhood were happy occasions. One, however, was a tragedy. There was a big sand pit with huge cliffs of sand where carts and lorries of builders and other sand users carried away sand. Obviously young children were not supposed to play in this sand-pit, but buckets and spades that were used at the seaside could not often be employed as the visits to the seaside were bound to be little more than once a year.

One fine summer evening some of the little children who lived near took their buckets and spades into the forbidden sand pit to play sand castles. Alas, a bank of sand collapsed on to them. The bigger ones struggled free and ran home raising the alarm, but two of the smallest lost their lives.

I remember the shock that this caused throughout the village and the horror that my sister and I felt when passing the beautiful, enticing sand of the sand-pit, and the puzzled wide-open eyes of a little friend of mine who had been in the sand pit at the time of the tragedy and could not, for weeks, fathom what had actually happened to her friends.

Games

Hop, Skip and Jump

Games were an endless fascination. practically none were organised games except on fine Friday afternoons. After compositions had been satisfactorily finished the older children went up the cleaves onto a patch of down and played rounders, while the younger children listened to a fairy story. Maisie was a good rounders player but I don't think I was. However, the games I refer to were those we played at playtime or before or after school. These seemed to have their seasons, though how or why they changed from one game to another is a mystery. There was bowling hoops, wooden for the girls and iron for the boys, hopscotch, whip top and skipping. Skipping was regarded as a girls' game and very few boys skipped. Two girls turned a long rope and other girls – sometimes as many as five – jumped into the rope and skipped together. Maisie was a champion skipper and at one of our Sunday School outings on the down she skipped something over two hundred steps with everyone standing around counting in disbelief that she could go on so long without making a mistake. She was wearing a pair of light brown shoes and at the end of this feat they were so soaked in perspiration that they turned into a muddy dark brown colour and never recovered.

Skipping Rhymes

We used our skipping prowess to find out who we should marry and what our wedding would be like. 'Tinker, tailor, soldier, sailor, rich man, poor man, beggar man, thief', struck me as a poor selection to choose from. Whatever happened to the much vaunted 'professions'. I suppose we were not expected to marry a doctor, a parson or a lawyer. Likewise 'coach, carriage, wheelbarrow, dung-cart' to convey the bride to her wedding was not much choice either. Hoots of laughter greeted the poor girl who had to go to her wedding in a dung-cart. Nobody ever thought of saying, 'Well, no thanks, I'd rather walk.' If, however, you were down to marry a thief and then found you would go to church in a carriage and wear silk (choice of 'silk, satin, muslin, rags'), it was obvious that your thief wasn't going to get found out. If you were to marry a rich man but found you had to go to the wedding in rags, our sympathy went out to the girl who was to marry such a skinflint.

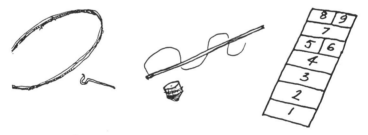

Hopscotch

Hopscotch was another favourite game. We drew a large chalk design on the asphalt surface of the playground or road and used a flat piece of tile to throw into each square in turn without touching any lines, and then hopped up and back without a foot touching the line.

At the top end you straddled the two shaded squares and then leapt around and came back again. Maisie and I and our friends were adept at this game. I am amazed when I look back at it now how very skilled it was.

Whip Top

Whip-tops was another favourite game and we used to whip ours up and down the road for hundreds of yards, which just goes to show how little traffic there was then. Some of my friends were content with a bit of string for the whip, but I used to steal my dad's leather laces and sent both my top and my rivals into a flat spin!

Ball on the Wall

We also played 'up on the wall' with rubber bouncing balls. This started with 'up the wall' – where the ball might be caught; then 'twist' – hands twisted; 'fold' – hands folded; ending with a complete turn around of the body before the ball might be caught. If you missed it, it was the next person's turn. We had a lot of beautiful big walls of old brick at the farm so this game seemed to go on in and out of the seasons of the others.

Swings

Swings were made by throwing a 'plough line', *i.e.* a rope used as a rein in ploughing, over the bough of an old apple tree in the orchard and making a swing in this way, but you needed to have a wooden seat or at least a thick hessian corn-sack to sit on to avoid getting a sore bottom! Maisie, working her legs backwards and forwards, could kick out and touch some leaves on the apple tree. I was less ambitious as the downward swing from a good height always made my tummy whiz around.

The Seasons

If you live on the land the seasons are not just dates on the calendar, they are the very stuff of life. City dwellers miss a lot of the variety of life by having the seasons somewhat ironed out by their environment and method of living. On cold frosty mornings we went to school stamping our feet to keep warm and slapping our gloved hands round our bodies, like two old men fighting, as my father always said. It was hard weather no doubt, but bracing, and sometimes there would be snow for playing snowballs or ice on puddles and ponds to be skated on if safe enough. Maisie and I enjoyed winter. The spring, with its smell of damp earth, flowers, blossoms and bird song needed no advocate. Summer, as we ran to school in muslin and sandals with the sun on our backs, was the light season – light in clothes and light in its long, long evenings. Autumn we waded in leaves almost up to our knees and kicked the lovely yellow, red and gold of them about with joyful abandon and, with pockets stuffed with apples and nuts, were totally unworried about the coming winter.

Primroses

The seasons very much ruled our lives and, of course, what had to be done on the farm and also what Maisie and I did. In the spring I remember going round to the local mill and mill-pond and down the stream's edge where the most beautiful primroses always grew. My mother warned us not to get too near the mill-pond, which I don't recollect being fenced off, though the footpath went right round it. Its brown, still depths always filled me with terror, but the path had to be traversed if you were to get the best primroses. There we picked huge bunches of the lovely pale yellow flowers and Maisie would not have them without some of the long green leaves. When we got home mother gave us a large shallow bowl and Maisie made an arrangement with a great mass of pale yellow flowers in the middle and a delightful fringe of green leaves. These we put on the hall table and it filled the entrance to the old farmhouse with beautiful subtle spring perfume.

Cowslipping was another matter. I certainly adored the cowslips and we picked bunches of them and made floral decorations with them, but mostly cowslips were taken to be the raw material for cowslip wine.

Bird's Nesting

The spring also brought bird's nesting. We went round the hedgerows, gardens and lanes and by careful observation found as many bird's nests as possible. We girls only whispered to each other where the nests were because there were still rampaging destroyers, yes, mainly male, who would come and take the eggs or pull the whole nest out if they knew about it. We watched the little birds and saw them making or visiting their nests – wrens, blackbirds, hedge-sparrows, thrushes, missel-thrushes, robins and a variety of tits abounded. If we found a nest we would not allow anyone to make a scamper up to it (*i.e.* a track where many feet had climbed up and down the bank and hedge) so that the nest could remain undisturbed.

Swallows and Plovers

A little later in the year swallows and swifts covered the eaves of our barn and the old Tudor house opposite with their mud-cemented nests. Whilst ploughing on the hill my father would sometimes cut into a plover's nest and then, with great regret he picked up the eggs and brought them home in his pocket. If they were fresh and did not have an embryo in them, we ate them fried for breakfast.

Pied Wagtails and Cuckoos

On a pouring wet spring day I spent hours watching, my nose pressed to the window pane, the 'polly dish-washers', *i.e.* the pied wagtails, splashing around and thoroughly enjoying the puddles. The cuckoo's call in April rang around the orchards, but when we found a hedge-sparrow's nest with a young cuckoo in it, and the hedge-sparrow's young dead on the ground around, Maisie and I shivered and shook and felt as if we were at the scene of a horrible crime. We found it impossible to come to terms with the cruelty of nature, but without it we knew our spring days would not be filled with the call of the cuckoo.

Pigeons

The cooing of the pigeons that my father hated and shot because of their destruction of the crops was neverthe-less something we always enjoyed. Their constant advice to the cattle thief to 'take two coos (cows), Taffy, take two coos, Taffy' amused us, and we mocked him. One day I climbed up a tree on which I could see a pigeon's nest, a sort of flat pile of sticks, and putting my hand over the edge felt two lovely pigeon eggs. I was overjoyed, but dropped rapidly to the ground and ran away in case the parent should find out the impertinence of my touching her children.

I Feed a Fledgling

A nest of fledglings was so obvious in our hedge that I could easily walk past and see the yellow rims of their gaping mouths open and begging for food. I had a sandwich, so I tore off a little bit of bread and dropped it into the gaping beak. I was horrified as I watched the fledgling trying to swallow it, and I thought it was going to choke there and then. I felt like a murderer, but then I saw it had got the bread down – but now I could see it through the skin of the young bird, inside it. In school I worried all day that I might have done dreadful harm to the little bird, but no, the brood seemed to continue satisfactorily their feathering and flew away. I never dropped any bread, or anything else, into a fledgling's beak again.

The Crow Mimic

Crows were not birds which we liked much. They were arrogant and cocky and destructive. They bossed us, rather than we bossing them – or even superiorly giving them room to live – as we did with other birds, but I came to have great respect for them. How did this fall out? Well, we used to rear chickens with broody hens, both Maisie and I did a lot of this. The old hen was clucking away at her chickens as she picked up the scattered corn and invited them to do likewise. It was then that I realised there was a crow picking up the corn and clucking in exact imitation of the hen. I could hardly believe it so I sat and watched and listened. I could not tell which clucking sounded more genuine, that of the hen or that of the crow. At last I called to Maisie and we both roared with laughter, saying, 'Oh, you clever old crow!', and never feeling quite so harshly about crows again.

Dancing the Polka

One other bird figured prominently in our childish lives. A little old lady lived in a bungalow (in those days of Empire, called a colonial type) with a verandah. She had a beautiful red coloured parrot in a cage swinging from the beams of the verandah. The old lady was something under five foot in height, slight in build and with a shock of unruly white hair, and she always wore capes, not coats. Picture the scene of Maisie and me watching her dancing for the parrot. She twirled round and round with her cape and hair flying whilst she sang in a creaky voice, "See me dance the polka, see me cover the ground, see my coat-tails flying as I turn my partner round." The bird was obviously so taken by this display that it too would dance in its cage and turn round and round on its perch. The old lady would say to Maisie and me, "Dance children, dance", and we would dance around in front of the parrot. Not, I think, without slight embarrassment of dancing before a bird.

Mushrooms

The seasons, as is their way, progressed each year through haymaking and harvest. If there had been rain, word went round the village that there were mushrooms 'on the hill'. Jacky Smith had filled his mother's washing basket full, and so on. There would be a lot of talk all the evening; could Maisie and I get up at crack of dawn and, armed with baskets, go with Dad up the steep chalk road to the down to gather mushrooms. On a few occasions we actually made it and were intrigued with the 'fairy rings' of mushrooms which we gathered with great glee. There were also lots of puffballs, but these neither we nor the other mushroomers gathered. We kicked them and watched the green spores scatter everywhere. Up on the down Father had to keep our direction for it would have been easy to get lost. We were told not to go anywhere near Sky Farm, which was said to be haunted. The rumour was that you could never close any of the doors; if you did, they just flew open again. Obviously a draught-loving ghost, or perhaps just built by a builder who could not hang doors. It sent a chill through us if we were in that part of the down, but perhaps that was the misty of drizzly early morning.

Lovely Food

We came back sometimes with a couple of baskets full, but sometimes we arrived too late and came home with only a few handfuls of mushrooms in each basket. Whichever way it was, we would be hungry and Mother would fry rashers of bacon and some of the washed and peeled mushrooms would be fried in the fat. We thought the field mushrooms were the best food we ever tasted. There were, of course, no cultivated mushrooms in the village in those days. Also we were so hungry after the long, early walk that I suppose almost anything would have been delicious.

Picking Watercress and Counting the Church Steps

Local chalk streams were justifiably famous for their watercress and although I doubt if the industry had begun to develop to anything like the level which a few years later it became, it was, at least, just beginning. We children did not know anything about this, but we did know that good watercress grew in the Coombe stream. So that any month with an 'r' in it we waded into the freezing water and picked bundles of watercress. We learnt exactly which water plants to pick and which to leave, of course, and mainly went for the little brown-tinged cresses, making up little bunches and carrying them home for our tea.

After picking the cress we dried our freezing toes and put on our socks and shoes again and had a session 'counting the church steps' guaranteed to warm anyone's feet. The church steps run right down one side of the valley and up the other and there are said to be 212 steps. If there were half a dozen of us we could never manage to arrive at the same figure for the steps, nor the same figure that we had counted last time. This did not worry us; we took it for granted that the holiness or magic of the church steps meant they altered slightly in number from time to time. Of course, adults thought they cannot really have done so but we knew they did. It probably depended on which one you started and ended.

Blackberrying

The late summer and early autumn was the time for gathering the various hedgerow fruits and nuts. Maisie and I always went blackberrying with a gang of girls, friends and cousins, always taking care to include a few tall ones with crook sticks to get at the higher branches. We each carried chip baskets and, thus armed, we tackled the hedges in the grassy meadows. At lunch-time we sat on the grass and ate 'doorsteps' of bread and farmhouse cheddar cheese, washed down with Mother's homemade lemon barley water. The hot afternoon under the hedges would test one's endurance but we persisted and went home by five o'clock with little baskets filled with blackberries in each hand. Mother was a wonderful jam maker and produced the most delicious blackberry jelly. As September crept along towards its end, we would snatch a few more blackberries to make blackberry and apple pies and puddings, but Mother always reminded us, "Don't pick blackberries after Michaelmas (29th September) because the devil puts his foot on them that day and they are no longer any use." Well, if you like to test this for yourself you will discover that they are well past their best by that time. With the record number of blackberries that we picked and ate we certainly saved the devil a devil of a lot of smart stepping!

Nutting

Nutting was another autumnal joy and mostly this meant gathering hazel nuts. We climbed up the hedges and got in amongst the green clusters of nuts. They should be picked just as the nuts are ripe enough to fall off their green calyxes. Not an easy moment to judge – too early and they would not part company with the calyx, the bitterness of which sets your teeth on edge when you come to bite it; too late and the nuts had shed out and then you had to pick them off the ground and compete with the squirrels and other little animals.

'Nuts' to our Business Effort

We were picking, cracking and eating hazel nuts one day in the hedge next to the village tennis courts, when one of the players, a rather lah-dee-dah young man, came over to us.

"Are those nuts good?", he demanded.

"Oh, yes" we said.

"Then bring me a few pounds to my house." A few pounds! That ought to be worth quite a few pennies, we thought. We gathered half-a-dozen kids and filled a big straw bag with nuts, six pounds, I believe. Together we presented ourselves on the gentleman's doorstep, ringing the bell with great abandon. A smart and rather lah-dee-dah lady appeared in the hall.

"What do you children want?", she inquired.

"We've come with the gentlemen's hazel nuts. He ordered them'" we announced. I remember to this day how she took a nut out and, putting it on the tiled floor, stepped on it with the not inconsiderable weight of her plump body. The nut cracked and splattered and went flat all over the floor-tile.

"These nuts are not ripe, not ripe at all", she said, and sent us packing!

Stained Faces

We always had lots of walnuts from the huge old walnut tree in the lower orchard by the pigsties. So walnutting was not an expedition, you just had to pick them or pick them up. During the walnut season our hands and faces would be stained brown with the green casings of the walnuts. I said I would tell you about the day we decided to turn ourselves into gypsies for a day. All of that Saturday morning we squeezed and rubbed the green walnut casings over our faces, proudly looking at our faces in the mirror to see how brown we were. Then, taking off our shoes and putting on our oldest pinnies, we went round to the hen houses and, carefully knocking at the doors, offered to sell them our imaginary clothes pegs. When the time came for going to bed, the most vigorous soaping and flannelling would not remove the stain. We had to go to Sunday School the next day in our spotless white, spotted muslin dresses, but appearing over the top of them those brown stained gypsy faces!

Sunday School Picnic

Sunday School at the charming seventeenth century chapel was a joyful and busy place, with lots of singing, acting and playing. Even if it did involve attending Sunday morning service and sitting as still as possible for an hour – a whole hour, and enduring an, at that time, totally meaningless sermon. When things became intolerable, Maisie and I sat in the bottom of the box pew at Mum and Dad's feet and made rabbits from our handkerchiefs. Only if the rabbit making became too obstreperous did Dad nudge us with his foot and Mum 'shush' us.

Sunday always seemed to me, as a child, the day when we exhibited our belief that cleanliness was next to Godliness. Having had a bath and hairwash the night before, we were dressed in clean clothes from top to bottom, before going to chapel. It was so much more difficult to achieve cleanliness in those days when water was carried from a pump or a well (or a rain water butt) and heated in a copper or over a kitchen range and washing clothes was something that occupied a whole day every week for a family. It was obviously a struggle to end up perfectly clean on Sunday. I regarded it as climbing the good people's ladder, having got to the cleanliness rung one might easily hop smartly onto the Godliness rung, but it must be more difficult to know if one had arrived!

Going to Sunday School was great fun, where we played in sand trays, did drawings and listened to Bible stories, many of which seemed as far-fetched as Red Riding Hood and the Wolf (Jonah and the Whale for example). Later, when we were older, the stories and reading became more serious, but they did not often have beneficial fall-out; ours however did. We were devoted to our teacher, when in the 1st. Class Girls, and she apparently to us. She worked at the village shop and if we went in during the dinner hour when the other ladies who ran the shop were at lunch, and asked for a penny-worth of humbugs or other sweets our teacher would fill the lovely brass pan of the scale until it went down with a wonderful sounding bump and we went away with a beautiful fat bag of sweets. Needless to say we always went sweet shopping during the dinner hour!

Summertime meant the Sunday School outing and my father lent his wagons to take children up on to the hill. Some twenty or so children would sit on the floor of the wagon whilst it jolted up the Castle Hill to the spot where the jollifications were held, just above the White Horse. Not only were the children taken up there, but all the paraphernalia of the feast, tea-urns and fresh water. I think the urns must have sat on primus stoves – certainly they produced masses of hot sweet tea. Long trestle tables were set up and covered with white tablecloths and laden with bread and butter, fish paste and jam, seed cake and sticky currant buns. Jellies and blancmange, too, had been carefully carried to the hill top. We had such a blow-out. The village ice-cream man filled up his 'stop me and buy one' tricycle on purpose for our feast. Sports and swinging boats followed. We slid down the steep sides of the prehistoric barrows, the long grass making a wonderful slide after one or two goes. Running on the short, springy, sheep-cropped turf was a joy I have not experienced elsewhere, and the blue harebells everywhere proclaimed this a chalk-given sward. The journey home in the wagon was all that we could by then manage, more asleep than awake, creaking and bumping down the hill.

Sunday School Anniversary

Sunday School Anniversary practice at the Yew Trees was a feature of spring and early summer evenings, when we went into the large and beautiful old garden at the back of the house to do our practice of recitations, little songs and plays. The huge trees stood out on the large green lawn where our teacher trained us for Anniversary Services and the balmy air, albeit full of midges, accompanied these efforts. We seemed such small children under these huge trees, but if we could learn to lift up our heads and throw out our voices in the open air, we could be sure that on Sundays we would be clearly heard right at the far corner of the gallery. The chapel was full of flowers on Anniversary Sunday, mainly white 'pinks', and the smell of these flowers has always reminded me of our recitations and songs. I think I can fairly say that Maisie and I never forgot our words although some very young children were struck dumb by the awe of the occasion and had to be helped out.

The Limits of Teetotalism

At school we were all encouraged to sign the pledge, that is, to sign that one would not drink alcohol or brandy as a medicine. I remember saying, 'Oh, that was lovely', when given some whisky in hot water with sugar when I had a cold. In spite of this apparent adherence to teetotalism, natural products and common sense attitudes seemed to reign in relation to this principle. For instance, my father always gave his men a mug of beer when they were working at hot dirty jobs, like haymaking, harvest or threshing. Natural products seemd to be excluded from the ban, such as home-made cider, wines and mead. Some of these may have been quite alcoholic but they were drunk without qualms. It was a great joke that anyone getting drunk on mead staggered backwards instead of forwards. I can't say I ever saw this extraordinary phenomenon happen. Of course my mother and father never went to the pub, but it always surprised me even as a child, that our principles could be so comfortably flexible.

Missionaries and Magic Lanterns

Missionaries and magic lanterns were inseparably linked in our young lives. I thought the missionaries must be beautifully brass-bound like the lanterns and certainly they had the same smell! Money was endlessly being sought for missionaries who went to far-off countries, particularly China, India or Africa, and from time to time they returned to give us magic lantern shows of these exotic countries. The lovely old magic lanterns were intriguing in themselves and their pictures were a fascinating travelogue which we could see nowhere else at the time. There was one old missionary who used to find the rows of fidgetting children a distraction and with a quaint mispronuciation used to say petulantly, "Don't figget children, don't figget", and we would say to each other, "Go on, figget, figget". In spite of the beautiful brass magic lantern and the flickering shadows on the screen, I stopped all my attendance at these shows after hearing about some Chinese coolies who had to come forward and have their heads cut off, not, I hasten to add, by the missionaries. I could no longer endure the horrors of these strange countries. My sister, I believe, was tougher and went on supporting them.

Christmas

Classy Christmas Puddings
As the year rolled to its end, Maisie and I planned and worked for Christmas. To start with, our school class made a large number of Christmas puddings. They were taken home and cooked by our governess and sent to poor people living in the East End of London. When I think back on it now, it must have been an enormous feat of organisation to get children of ages between nine and fourteen to do this. First of all everyone's sleeves were rolled up and everyone's hands and nails scrubbed. Then on the long school benches covered with clean white paper, currants were picked over, sultanas washed and raisins stoned. Crusty cottage loaves were reduced to breadcrumbs. Suet bought in a large piece from the butcher was finely chopped. Eggs were beaten, flour sifted, nutmegs grated and lemons juiced. In the end it all come together in a huge mixing bowl, at which we lined up to give it a lucky stir and make a lucky wish. Then it was spooned into umpteen little basins and each tied with a spotless pudding cloth. We all enjoyed the Christmas pudding making and I think we must all have been on our best behaviour for it. Certainly our governess's control of her children took on an almost miraculous effect at that time.

A Fiery Father Christmas

The Sunday School always had its Christmas Party and feast. Tea being not dissimilar to that which had taken place 'up on the hill' in the summer, except that now it was firmly protected from the rough winter elements by being in the warm Sunday School room with the scrubbed wooden floor. The floor about which my aunt once said, "It is scrubbed as white as a pastry board?" After the meal we had, in the past, always had a huge Christmas tree. Standing in the centre of the room it reached the ceiling and was lit by dozens of little candles; it was laden with presents for every child there and Father Christmas handed them out. But one year this beautiful scene fell over into one of terror.

Maisie and I suppose fifty to sixty other children were waiting for our presents when Father Christmas caught the jacket of his red suit trimmed with cotton wool on a lighted candle. It flared up into a huge blaze, completely engulfing the man inside. The youngest of us thought this was all part of the Christmas play-acting and perhaps because of this there was no panic amongst the children. A quick-thinking adult guest enveloped Father Christmas in his overcoat and rolled him over onto the ground, but the poor man was very badly burnt and we never had a Christmas tree afterwards. In following years our presents were given out in other ways, such as from Santa in a sleigh, or from a wishing well, where one's presents were attached by someone down the 'well' when the spoken wish was made.

Dad's Feast

At home, Christmas was indeed a feast, my father being very fond of good food. His heart's desire was a huge roast of beef followed by an enormous Christmas pudding. No turkeys for us I am afraid, but once I remember us having a huge goose. What was left behind from the goose was a great mass of goose-grease (*i.e.* the fat from the roasting) and a bony Christmas ghost. Goose-grease was regarded by the older country people as a marvellous cure-all. If you had bronchitis it was rubbed into your chest. If you had backache it was rubbed into your back, and so on. My mother swore she would never again have a Christmas goose; presumably the thought of all that rubbing to dispose of this bonanza was too off-putting.

A Bony Ghost

The old farmhouse in which we lived was huge and barn-like, and it even had a secret room – a small room next to our bedroom, the window of which had been filled in and the door wallpapered over. Small wonder, if on winter nights when the only light upstairs was flickering candles, that we thought of ghostly former inhabitants. Shortly after the 'goosey' Christmas, Maisie and I went to bed, and in the unheated bedroom we undressed with enormous speed and leapt into our warm feather beds. We blew out our candle and lay ready to sleep when 'knock, knock, scrape, scrape' sounded overhead. We rushed to the stairs and called,

"Dad, there is somebody upstairs."

Father came up and went into all the rooms, but no-one was there.

"Perhaps it's a ghost', we said, but by then we were so tired that we just went off to sleep. When our parents came to bed they also heard the 'scrape, scrape, knock, knock' intermittent but persistent from their room. Oh well, my father wasn't going to let any old ghost keep him awake. Ghosts could wait until morning – and he went to sleep. In the morning, Dad climbed up into the roof-space and there found a huge goose bone which had obviously been carried there by a rat. It was the rat's efforts to tug this bone through a crack too narrow for it which gave us our only real 'ghost'.

A Potato in our Stockings

Christmas meant decorating the lower floors of the house with coloured paper chains mostly made by Maisie and me at school. Father had a cousin living in China and I think it must have been from them that we acquired a mass of lovely Chinese lanterns. Mistletoe which grew on one or two of our apple trees was our favourite Christmas plant. I don't remember any holly being used and we never had a family Christmas tree. Presents were given, small ones in our stockings (these were long, plain, woollen or cashmere stockings presumably of mother's or grandmother's). In addition to the small presents would be oranges, nuts, figs and dates. It was the only day of the year we were allowed to eat sweets before breakfast. Larger presents, only one each, were given after breakfast. Once Dad played a cruel joke on Maisie and me. Knowing we had got beyond the stage of believing in Father Christmas, he put a huge potato in the toe of each stocking. We thought it must be something wonderful and even took a bite of it in the dark of our early Christmas morning stocking finding. When we discovered that the extra big stocking present was indeed a potato we were furious and took them to the door of our parents' bedroom and threw them repeatedly at the door with such a crashing and a banging that their Christmas Day started very early that year!

Hide and Seek in the Dark

Our cousins often came for Christmas and other holidays and, with friends, we might then be seven or eight children. On winter evenings we adored the game of 'hide and seek in the dark'. The barny old house, dimly lit with gas downstairs and not at all upstairs meant that we could find dozens of places to hide in its five bedrooms, two staircases and half-a-dozen cupboards and glory-holes. The moonlight streamed through the window as shadowy figures took up their hiding places. The child who was 'it' down in the hall counted laboriously to one hundred, then yelled out 'coming' and tore through the house to find the hidden children. Once you were found you had to come out from under the bed, on top of the wardrobe, or whatever it was and gather in the hall to see who had resisted the seeker longest on this occasion.

Once I opened the cellar door in mistake for a cupboard door and fell down a whole flight of twenty steps into a dark and spooky cellar. I yelled, and several people came and carried me back upstairs. I was unhurt, but scared, and my hiding place had been ruined for that night.

Sometimes Maisie and I and two or three others would all try to squash into one closet. One would say to the others, "Sshh, don't breathe so loud, you'll give the game away. You better not sneeze or we'll shove you out the door." The seeker would stand in the long dark passage to the kitchen and listen for such whisperings. We held our breath as the seeker went by, sometimes ending by bursting out laughing, and the irate seeker would say, "Oh you silly things, you spoilt the whole game. Go and play ludo."

In the summer, outdoor 'hide and seek' allowed us to use the stables, cow shed, barn and other outbuildings. It did not take place in the pitch darkness as with the indoor game, but the seeker could finish counting and look round the farmyard with not a child in sight and no sound of one. It might well be past supper-time before everyone was found.

Valued Animals and Precious Characters

Animals Our Constant Companions

Living on a farm I never had any of the sentimental views of animals I discovered later in many towns-people. The animals were simply just about the most important creatures in our lives and were always treated as such. The welfare of the horses, the cows, the sheep and all the other animals was something we were equally responsible for and so we kept our eyes open for any lameness or other sickness and reported it at once. We knew, of course, that some animals would end up being killed and did not grieve over this, probably because their lives were meanwhile good, comfortable and natural. This early feeling has, no doubt, always fuelled my dislike of factory farming.

Pig Killing

At certain times of the year, particularly in autumn, pig-killing went on in the yards of farms. On our way to school or back we would hear a pig squealing. We knew that a pig was being killed and some of us would run to see the blood let out or the bristles burnt off. I have to confess that Maisie and I didn't quite have enough courage to do this, but for all that we were not a bit squeamish about eating animals we had known daily. We saw the pig cut up to become sides of bacon, hams and gammons and the insides to be patiently washed and become liver, brawn, chitterlings, faggots and sausages. All of which we loved. The fleck or fat was cut up and rendered down to become a soft lard and lovely little frizzly bits called scraps, which we children ate with gusto. We also sometimes had our toast spread with lard and sprinkled with salt – delicious! (It was nothing like the lard you now buy in shops.) No doubt this fare would horrify present day dietitians, as I suppose would also our sweet and squelchy lardy-cakes. We felt that animals were happy companions in life and afterwards obliged us with good food for our care of them. I feel this is the way it should be.

Horses

Maisie and I loved most of the farm animals. Incredible as it seems now, my father had eleven horses. Ten were shires and one was a trap-horse. There were two stable ranges, only one man was called 'carter'; he was the chief horseman, but the other men also helped clean the stables, take care of the horses and, of course, took the horses out hauling and ploughing.

Maisie and I used to rummage around in the stables and find the fancy brasses and coloured and tasselled ear-caps that they must have worn in some smart parade. Usually we saw them going 'up on the hill', one horse tied to the tail of the one in front and the carter sitting on the front horse, his straw bag of lunch and the horses' nose-bag hanging on the hames. On autumn and winter mornings Carter left with his horses just as it was getting light. He returned in the evening just as it was getting dark. He had been ploughing all day.

Ploughman's Lunch
Sometimes I went with my father to visit him about lunch-time and sat with wonderment as he ate the whole bottom of a cottage loaf, a huge lump of cheddar cheese and a large Spanish onion. He had a large sharp pocket knife and was methodical in his eating. He sliced a piece of bread, then a slice of cheese to sit on it and finally topped it off with a slice of onion. This went on inexorably until the whole lot was gone and washed down with sweet cold tea from an enamel can.

The Bull
Maisie and I loved the horses, the cows, the sheep, the pigs and even the squawky hens. Two animals filled us with fear. One was the bull. When he was brought out of his shed with the men holding him by a pole attached to a ring in the end of his nose, tensions seemed to mount and we hid out of sight. Nothing untoward ever happened with our bull, but a few years later when I was a teenager working on a farm in North Devon, our neighbouring farmer was killed by his own bull. It was a holiday and all the men were away from the farm,

so when the bull broke out he tried putting it back into the shed by himself with disastrous results.

A Wild White Wyandotte

My mother bought a very special white wyandotte cock who lorded it over all the hens in the yard. I, at the age of eight, walked out amongst his hens and the fierce cock flew at me knocking me down flat on the ground. I yelled and those who came to rescue me couldn't stop laughing to think that I had been knocked down by a cock. This was the only other animal beside the bull of which I was afraid.

Sozzled Cock

Some years later when I was visiting a Devon farm I was taken over to see the huge 'hog's heads' of cider in the cider store, and to taste the cider.

"How do you make it so good?", I asked the farmer.

"Well, our best apples go into it of course, but if you have a bad-tempered old cock around the farmyard pick him up and drop him in the barrel, feathers and all."

Could I believe him, I wondered? It seemed poetic justice on bad-tempered old cocks.

Fishing for Tiddlers

The little chalk stream of Stradbrook which wound its way through the village was the home of sticklebacks, minnows and other tiny fish, usually called tiddlers. Maisie and I and other friends used to spend mornings fishing. First we had to go and dig up a can full of worms to use as bait. Then we made a fishing rod, a piece of black cotton on a long stick with a bent pin on the end of the cotton. A large jam jar with string tied round the top and made into a handle completed the fishing tackle. Then we set off for the stream. When we arrived at the stream's bank we could see all sorts of lovely little fish darting about in the clear water. Some with red sides which we called 'redbreasts' and some with very large heads which we called 'loggerheads'. First we impaled the poor worms on the pin and then we cast our cotton line most professionally into the stream, competing to see who could cast the farthest. At the appearance of this unwonted largess some poor little fish would take a bite and then, 'hey presto', it was airlifted out of the stream and dropped into our awaiting large jam jar. Occasionally we would see a beautiful royal blue kingfisher dart over the stream, no doubt anxious to know who was stealing his food supply.

Cold Water

One other watery occasion took place when I was a few years older and had just started at high school. I was perched in a hazel bush which leant out over the stream imitating a cuckoo when the branch broke. I fell right down into the about three feet of water, soaking my new school uniform of a navy blue coat and navy blue serge tunic. I had to rush home as quickly as possible and get these heavy garments dried and pressed ready for school next morning. That taught me one lesson; the lesson I learned from fishing was not to do it, as the little fish always died after we got home.

Our life as children did not include much dealing with water or boats and boating (other than trips to the Isle of Wight or around the bay in the *Skylark*, when we went on our annual holiday to Bournemouth). From time to time we went rowing on the lake at Edington, which in those days was a Tea Garden so that one could first have tea outdoors and then go for a row on the old monastery lake. Maisie and I enjoyed this very much although it was my brother who was the oarsman, but I never had and never have got used to the wobbliness which occurs when you step into a rowing boat. We were definitely not water babies, much preferring play on dry land. However, I have here to make a confession about one summer evening when Maisie and I and, I think, my cousins, found an old whitewash bucket with pump attached which had been used for whitewashing farm buildings. We filled it with water and hid behind the hedge. When the local bus went past with its windows open (it was a hot evening) we pumped away and squirted somewhat limey water in the open windows of the bus and were rewarded with the shrieks of the occupants. Nobody presumably knew how the water had suddenly squirted out from behind the hedge.

Gentleman Jack
One of our favourite haunts on the way home from school was at the workshop of 'Gentleman Jack' the cabinet maker. He was called this, I suppose, because of his very smart appearance, neat hair and smart

clothes over which he wore a carpenter's white apron. But perhaps also because of his very pleasant manner. He was always patient with us children who crowded his workshop, and told us what he was doing. We watched his handling and working, with consummate skill, the wood into household furniture. We picked up the lovely smelling curly shavings from the floor and hung them like ringlets around our hats, whilst Jack planed, glued and stained all manner of things. Then we, tiring of the concentration of watching such skill, just upped and went home, our wooden ringlets waving in the breeze.

The Bird Scarer

The problem of keeping the birds off sown corn, especially rooks and crows, was as much a problem to farmers in the 1920's as it had ever been, and was before the period of the automatic cartridge scarers; scarecrows only had a limited effectiveness. When we were children the crow scaring was done by a young man who was born with less well developed ability than most of the rest of us thought we had. 'Funny Jack' was his name. He would be employed for a few pence to sit in the field for hours on end and whizz around a rattle or a pair of clackers, interspersed with a few well chosen shouts of 'Hoy!', 'Clear off!', etc. My father would go out to the field during the morning and maybe again in the afternoon and let off his double-barrelled shotgun a few times just to give the poor lad moral support and the crows a few hot behinds. How successful these efforts were I do not know but undoubtedly the crow scarer would have lost his important job in life if it had not been carried out.

The Blacksmith

The Blacksmith's shop was another centre of attraction for some of us children. The hissing of hot iron as it was plunged into water and the smoking, pungent smell of horses' hoofs burning as the new shoe was being fixed, were always present as we passed the Smith's open-fronted forge. The Smith was a large man eternally busy. The horses were huge and awaiting patiently or restlessly this necessary attention to their feet. I always felt they were undergoing a minor operation, as we did when we were taken to the dentist and did not hang around the Smith's hissing, banging, pungent smoking shop to embarrass them any longer than I could help.

The White Horse

The Westbury White Horse, that I have mentioned in passing before, was the great chalk white horse cut out in the turf on the escarpment just below Bratton Castle, and immediately adjoined land then rented by my father. Maisie and I and friends or cousins often did an expedition up to the White Horse and took our tea there for a picnic. The aim of the most agile and oldest children was to climb all the way round the outline of the chalk cut of the horse. It was very steep and a long way round. We started at the ear and I would brave my lack of a head for heights and go and sit on the eye then, encouraged still further, I might walk down around the nose or the two front legs. Others meanwhile would probably be half way round the horse, but when you were almost up to the back again you had to face the enormous test of character of going all the way round the tail. Some of us skipped it amid jeers and others tackled it amid cheers. When we got back to the ear again, tea and sandwiches never tasted so good. Our White Horse was (and is) a homely old nag and not a bit like that beautiful if fearsome 'Picassoesque' white horse at Uffington. We were told in school that it was put there to mark the victory of King Alfred over the Danes in 878, though a date as recent as the eighteenth century seems more likely.

Village Characters

In my childhood I think people were and appeared to be far more variable in look and character than they are today. There was not the ubiquitous small car or the handy clothes bought off the peg from Marks and Sparks. Except perhaps for the young chaps who poured out of Reeves' Ironworks, almost all wearing flat caps and bib and brace overalls, the variety of dress amongst the other villagers was very noticeable.

At this time also, transport varied too. A lot of people rode bikes, others walked whilst still others used pony traps and other horse-drawn vehicles. Some elderly people were still dressed in Victorian clothes. My grandmother, for example, dressed just as Queen Victoria had done on her Diamond Jubilee, with bonnet tied with black silk ribbons, cape fastened at the neck and a skirt sweeping the ground. Unfortunately she always believed somebody was trying to sneak off with her reels of cotton and so she hid them in the turned up rim of her bonnet. There were times, of course, when she forgot to remove them and went off to her devotions with white, pink and blue cotton reels nestling in the back of her bonnet rim!

Several other characters were most decidedly Edwardian in appearance. Two brothers and a sister who drove up and down the village several times a day in a high pony-trap were such. The men had bowler hats and thick tweed suits of a vintage some twenty years previous, and the elderly maiden sister a high-necked black blouse and a large straw hat. We youngsters used sometimes to be given a ride in this perilous vehicle and sometimes, even more perilously, we just hung on out of sight at the back with our arms fit to break and our legs flying in the air.

Another odd couple who inhabited a little thatched cottage must have been just like Jack Spratt and his wife, since she was very, very fat, and he was very, very thin. Nobody, I imagine, ever had enough courage to ask if they ate off the same plate! The old man's clothes hung on him like a very thin scarecrow. He looked like the epitome of the very poor man. One day, however, when he was working at threshing (a casual job when he could get it, for he was not regularly employed), the other men ribbed him about really having a lot of money which he kept hidden under his bed. The devout old man replied to them by saying, "I be rich indeed, but not with this world's goods." One can imagine that that reply floored the young tormentors.

Maisie and I were always intrigued with one old man six feet two inches in height with a back like a ramrod who continually followed horses around his home streets with a shovel, wheel-barrow and broom to sweep up that good fertiliser the horse manure. He took it back to his cottage and put it on the two straight rows of large double daisies that ran each side of his path up to his front door. My father always said he had to have his daisies as they reminded him of his two rows of brass buttons he had always worn on his scarlet army tunic.

One old chap who always intrigued me went for a walk (on summer days) with a folding stool in his hand and was to be seen sitting at the roadside with his old yellowed straw hat with a blue and gold ribbon band fringing his pink and sweating face and cheerful smile. There was also a deaf farmer (or perhaps it was his wife who was deaf) who could be heard right across the valley shouting from the hillside to his wife at home, "I baint going to fall missis, I be as sure-footed as a goat." To my mind that was exactly what he looked like ranging on the hangings, those steep-sided slopes of the escarpment. Then there was the old countryman whose answer to my father's enquiry, "How be 'ee today Jarge?", was always, "I be, how be thee?" This was an answer which amazed and puzzled me for a very long time until I came across Hamlet's speech "To be or not to be, that is the question" ... so then it was an affirmation of one's determined tenacity of life – or something.

There was a sad reminder of the war in a poor young man who had to be pushed around the village in a blanketed bathchair by a military nurse – evidence of the smashing of young men by the guns of war. I always felt very sad when we passed him.

Newer type characters of that time were two young women who had started a poultry farm and went about their work in knee-breeches. Although these had been used by the Land Army during the war, they were the only women so clad in the village. If they shocked the older inhabitants I suppose so also did my rather older girl cousins, from that seat of fashion, Devizes, who came to stay for the summer holidays and, wearing their long strings of beads and cloche hats, danced the Charleston (when grandmother wasn't looking) and tried to teach it to Maisie and me.

In the chapel services there were still frock-coated old gentlemen aplenty, but the one whom Maisie and I used to watch with fascination was the one with the disappearing pince-nez. He sang vociferously during the hymns holding his hymn book at arms length, his pince-nez glasses perched on the end of his nose. At the end of the hymn he simply squeezed up his nose like a rabbit and the pince-nez fell off. We waited with bated breath for them to crash to the floor; alas, this never happened for they were evidently secured by a long and invisible chain. The possibility that this might one day happen always sustained our interest.

Fires and Fire Engines

One evening in spring whilst swinging from swings in the apple tree in the top orchard, Maisie and I heard such a mass of voices raised that we wondered what could be happening in the centre of the village. Then, billowing smoke told us there must be a fire, although I must point out there was often billowing smoke from perfectly well controlled bonfires. However, we heard such a clatter and such a cacophony of voices that it was obvious this was no bonfire. It was indeed the Bratton Fire Engine being taken out to do its duty at a thatch fire. This fire-engine had a sort of composite handle at which three or four people stood each side and pumped up and down to draw water from a tank or stream to send a jet up onto the thatch of the burning roof. After numbers of people had tried slinging up pails of water which did not reach the base of the chimney stack where the fire was, even this primitive machine was a help.

Considering the number of thatched roofs that existed in those days, and the fact that many people had oil lamps and candles in their houses and open fires in their grates, it is surprising that in our childhood I only remember this one thatched roof fire. People must have been very, very careful with their lamps and fires. The ancient fire-engine and swarms of villagers did manage to do the trick and put out the burning thatch, so that by the time the modern fire-engine arrived from Westbury or Trowbridge the locals could boast through their dirt and sweat that all was under control. But these *real* firemen had to get up on the roof with their little hatchets and hack off lots of the thatch which had been saved just to show, I suppose, that they had not come for nothing. We children went home and chattered excitedly to our parents about the great fire we had seen, though it was really a fairly puny fire.

However, I do remember one which was not. That was a fire at what must have been an old woollen mill and was at that time a building yard and store of all sorts of wooden material. This was one of the fiercest fires I ever saw in my life. Nobody knew how it started. We children and half the village population stood in the nearby roadway and watched whilst the flames licked and tore at the piles of sawdust and shavings and stacks of timber and even at the stone building and then exploded with great bursts. The poor communal efforts of the hand pump machine would have been useless on this occasion and I cannot remember that even the town brigades were more successful.

Looking into Reeves's Works

In the centre of Bratton village was situated the big foundry and agricultural equipment works belonging to R. & J. Reeves and Son. This made and repaired sll sorts of agricultural machinery. Ploughs, for which they were justly famous, threshing machines, carts and a great variety of other equipment. We children used to run up Carpenter's Shop Lane on the way to and from school and peer in, perhaps through a broken feather board, and watch the men working. They were mainly fathers of our friends and knew us quite well. We would see them painting new ploughs in bright blue paint or carts with blue in the main body and orange wheels. My friend's father was one of the paint shop men. He was a nice man with a very bushy moustache and I had often been into his cottage after work and seen him assiduously washing his moustache to get the paint out of it. After seeing the episode we used to shout through the peep hole, 'Hello, Mr. Smith, have you got paint in your moustache?', and so embarrassing the poor man. I suppose some paint sprinkled off the brush when, for instance, wheel spokes were being painted, but I thought the paint brush and the moustache so much resembled each other that one might actually be used to help the work of the other!

We also used to stand upon piles of stones and gawp in the fitters' shop, particularly where the young apprentices worked, who had so recently been our fellow students at school. We called their names but disappeared jolly quick if any senior men turned up. We soon tired of seeing the lathes turning and ran off to pry into something else.

The Reeves's hooter dominated the life of the village; in the morning, at lunch time and in the evening. If we were not home for tea before the five o'clock hooter went there would be ructions. So sometimes the sound of the hooter saw us flying down the lanes like race horses as we realised we had dawdled just too long.

Shopping Visits to Town

Our shopping visits to town were very rare occasions. This must have been because almost all of our clothes were home-made by Mother and almost the only things left to buy were boots for the winter and sandals for the summer, and, I suppose, waterproof hats and coats. I remember lots of times when Maisie and I were hauled up to stand by Mother's treadle sewing machine whilst she measured us from top to toe for some garment. When, however, a shopping expedition was decreed we got on to the Saturday bus with Mother and went along to Westbury. It was an old red London open-topped bus and you could climb up the spiral staircase and look down on everybody as you passed by.

Arriving at the shops was for me decidedly less exciting, especially trying on shoes and boots and walking up and down in them. I never liked any of them and my Mother almost despaired. However, what I did enjoy was seeing the little containers of money shot from the side of the shop to the cash office and sometimes right upstairs to the next floor. Then the change and the receipts were shot back again to be delivered to the customer. I longed to be able to pull these handles and have a wonderful time shooting the boxes around the wires. When we got home that day all our play would be of taking money and shooting the change back in little boxes. Of course imagination had to take over as we had no wonderful mechanisms at home.

War and Peace

At the time of which I write, the War Office, as it was
then called, did not control our part of the Plain. I give
the following two examples of the week-end manoeuvres,
and the Peace Play, to show what the feelings of at least
a section of Bratton village was in the twenties. It was,
I would say, one of shock from the Great War and
determination to avoid war in the future. Although
these feelings had not yet become overtly pacifist, they
impressed themselves even on our childish conscious-
ness.

One Military Invasion
Although we were so near military bases on Salisbury
Plain at Larkhill and elsewhere, we were, down that
edge of the Plain, far enough not to have perpetual
contact with them. I do remember though one weekend
when hundreds, it seemed like thousands, of soldiers
descended on the village. They made their camp in one
of my father's grassy meadows, the Great Ground. We
children wandered around among them and watched
their cooks cutting up huge sides of beef and making
stew on their large camp cooking stoves. They had no
tents and seemed to shelter their beds with a thick grey
blanket thrown over poles. I remember thinking how
wet they would get if it rained in the night.

Shining Soldiers

We children stood by and gawped too as they marched smartly through the village with polished brasses and shiny boots and very smartly pressed uniforms. This must have been about 1925 and I soon discovered that there was an air of great coolness towards the military. When they stayed over Sunday and turned our quiet Lord's Day into a football playing jamboree, it turned into hostility amongst the people I knew. Most of the chapel people were, I think, very anti-military and of course this period was near enough to the Great War to stir lots of sad memories. Fortunately, the soldiers melted away as quickly as they had come, and we children spent the next few days marching up and down the road like soldiers.

The Peace Play

Some year or two later than this our Governess told us we were going to do a Peace Play. She and her friends were writing it and we children would act it in a public performance on the stage of the Jubilee Hall. It was, in a simplified form, about the causes of the Great War. Different children took the parts of different countries. They were dressed in representations of national costume and had name sashes indicating their country around them. One large boy was dressed in a soldier's uniform with a sash saying 'WAR'. I was Peace and had a white dress and white diaphanous wings and a lovely blue sash saying 'PEACE'. It was really a plea for no more war, but for the League of Nations to be given a chance to settle disputes without resort to war. When I look back I find its message as important today as it was then, and I am glad I had such teachers.

Glossary

Barrows: Prehistoric burial mounds around Bratton Castle.

Beauty of Bath: Eating apple, ripe in July.

Big Room: School room with pupils ten to fourteen years old.

Binder (self-binder): Machine which cuts corn and ties sheaves with automatic cutter.

Binder-twine: Coarse string used in the binder and for many other purposes.

Bushel Baskets: Large two-handled basket made from withies.

Carter: A head horseman was 'the Carter'.

Castle Hill: Road up to Bratton castle, Iron Age hill fort.

Cleaves: Steep chalk paths up on the down.

Coping: Thatch along the walls of the sheep fold making for warmth and shelter.

Diddicoys: To us this just meant gypsies, but it is a Romany word for travellers.

Down barn: Group of barns and cottages on Salisbury Plain.

Drug-shoe: A metal shoe chained to a wagon body, put under the wheel as a brake.

Fold: Enclosure of wattle hurdles retaining sheep.

Gault: stratum of impervious clay underlying the greensand.

Governess: Head teacher at Bratton British School.

Hames: Brass or wood part of the horse's harness attached to the collar of a draught horse.

Hanging: The grassy escarpment that runs from the valley floor up to Salisbury Plain, particularly evident at 'The Coomb'.

Hare's form: The seat or the lie of a hare, usually in long grass, always above ground.

Hay-loader: Haymaking implement which was drawn behind a wagon and scraped up the hay and carried it up on to the wagon.

Hiles: Stooks usually made up of six or eight sheaves stood up to dry in the harvest field.

Hogshead: A very large wooden cask or barrel holding cider; the amount varied, but probably forty gallons.

Horse-rakes and side-rakes: Horse-drawn machines which raked the cut hay into wind-rows.

Lades: Removable racks mounted to front and back of wagon for bulky loads.

Lanes: Footpaths between the houses.

Milk-float: Light, two wheeled horse-drawn trap.

Orange Blenheims and Russets: Harder keeping apples.

Plough line: Rope used as rein in ploughing.

Sheaves: Bundles of corn tied by binder.

Shorthorn: Breed of cows common in Wiltshire herds at the time and usually of mixed colours.

Truckle bed: Iron bedstead on large castors.

Tynings: Belts of trees on Salisbury Plain.

Up the down: On Salisbury Plain.

EX LIBRIS PRESS publishes a range of books in the areas of History, Countryside, Walking Guides, Biography and Literature, mostly with a West Country flavour.

For a free, illustrated catalogue describing books currently in print please contact the publishers:
Ex Libris Press, 1 The Shambles,
Bradford on Avon, Wiltshire, BA15 1JS
Tel / Fax 0225 863595